Plant Parts

Leaves

Revised Edition

by Vijaya Khisty Bodach

Consulting Editor: Gail Saunders-Smith, PhD

Consultant: Judson R. Scott, Former President
American Society of Consulting Arborists

CAPSTONE PRESS
a capstone imprint

Pebble Plus is published by Capstone Press,
1710 Roe Crest Drive, North Mankato, Minnesota 56003.
www.mycapstone.com

Copyright © 2007, 2016 by Capstone Press, a Capstone imprint. All rights reserved.

No part of this publication may be reproduced in whole or in part, or stored in a retrieval system, or transmitted in any form or by any means, electronic, mechanical, photocopying, recording, or otherwise, without written permission of the publisher. For information regarding permission, write to Capstone Press, 1710 Roe Crest Drive, North Mankato, Minnesota 56003.

Library of Congress Cataloging-in-Publication Data is available on the Library of Congress website.

ISBN: 978-1-5157-4244-9 (revised paperback)
ISBN: 978-1-5157-4353-8 (ebook pdf)

Editorial Credits
Sarah L. Schuette, editor; Jennifer Bergstrom, designer; Kelly Garvin, photo researcher/photo editor

Photo Credits
Capstone Studio: Karon Dubke, Cover, 5; Shutterstock: Brooke Whatnall, 19, Bruce MacQueen, top left 22, David Litman, 17, Mike Kuhlman, 7, Mr Zap, 13, Myotis, bottom left 22, Roman Sigaev, 9, Romeo Koitmae, 1, Ryoma Kawasemi, 21, SusaZoom, 15, Werner Muenzker, right 22, WizData, Inc., 11

Note to Parents and Teachers

The Plant Parts set supports national science standards related to identifying plant parts and the diversity and interdependence of life. This book describes and illustrates leaves. The images support early readers in understanding the text. The repetition of words and phrases helps early readers learn new words. This book also introduces early readers to subject-specific vocabulary words, which are defined in the Glossary section. Early readers may need assistance to read some words and to use the Table of Contents, Glossary, Read More, Internet Sites, and Index sections of the book.

Table of Contents

Plants Need Leaves 4
All Kinds of Leaves 12
Eating Leaves. 16
Wonderful Leaves. 20

Parts of a Maple Tree 22
Glossary 23
Read More 23
Index 24
Internet Sites. 24

Plants Need Leaves

Leaves grow from
the stems of plants.
Most leaves are green.

Leaves make food
for the whole plant.
They use water, air,
and sunlight
to make the food.

Veins inside leaves
bring the food to the stem.
Stems carry the food
to the rest of the plant.

Leaves give off oxygen
when they make food.
We breathe oxygen.

All Kinds of Leaves

Thin pine tree leaves

look like needles.

They stay green

all year long.

13

Broad maple leaves
turn orange and yellow
in autumn.
They fall off the tree.
New leaves grow in spring.

Eating Leaves

Lettuce leaves make a tasty salad. Each head of lettuce has layers of leaves.

Giraffes eat only leaves. They spend most of the day biting leaves off treetops.

Wonderful Leaves

Broad or narrow,

soft or fuzzy,

leaves help plants stay alive.

Parts of a Maple Tree

seed

leaves

stem

leaves

stem

Glossary

oxygen—a colorless gas in the air; people and animals breathe oxygen

stem—the long main part of a plant that makes leaves; food made by leaves moves through stems to the rest of the plant

veins—the small tubes inside a leaf; veins carry food and water

Read More

Farndon, John. *Leaves.* World of Plants. San Diego: Blackbirch Press, 2005.

Freeman, Marcia S. *What Plant Is This?* Everything Science. Vero Beach, Fla.: Rourke, 2005.

Mattern, Joanne. *How Pine Trees Grow.* How Plants Grow. Milwaukee: Weekly Reader, 2006.

Index

air, 6

food, 6, 8, 10

lettuce, 16

maple leaves, 14

oxygen, 10

pine needles, 12

stems, 4, 8

sunlight, 6

veins, 8

water, 6

Internet Sites

FactHound offers a safe, fun way to find Internet sites related to this book. All of the sites on FactHound have been researched by our staff.

Here's how:

1. Visit www.facthound.com

2. Choose your grade level.

3. Type in this book ID 0736863443 for age-appropriate sites. You may also browse subjects by clicking on letters, or by clicking on pictures and words.

4. Click on the Fetch It button.

Facthound will fetch the best sites for you!

Word Count: 130
Grade: 1
Early-Intervention Level: 15